Step by Step (

Manoeuvres

With a supplementary bonus section on

Show Me Tell Me

By Debbie Brewer

Contents:

Supplementary Bonus:

Show Me Tell Me Questions

Introduction:

As an Approved Driving Instructor, I regularly teach manoeuvres to my pupils enabling them to become skilled at reversing and turning the car in various situations whilst keeping themselves and everyone one around them safe and with minimal inconvenience. While doing so, I have often been asked to write down simple sets of instructions in a step by step form to help them understand how to perform the manoeuvre. Some find it helpful to take home and refer to when they are practicing in their own cars. Some find that just by re-reading how they did the manoeuvre in the lesson helps embed that new knowledge into their memories.

As an Ordit registered Instructor Trainer, I have also been asked many times by other instructors (ADIs) how I teach manoeuvres to my pupils. There are many different methods for teaching manoeuvres available, but those listed here are the ones I have found most useful.

However you decide to use this guide, I hope its simple step by step approach, and its section on essential hints and tips helps you to understand and improve, and enables you to perform manoeuvres more safely and skilfully in the future.

Essential Hints and Tips:

At what speed should I do my manoeuvres?

You will find that the slower you perform the manoeuvre, the easier it becomes, because you give yourself time to be more accurate with your thinking and steering. Remember the clutch control and speed you use when you are 'peeping and creeping' out of a closed junction? It is this same speed and same clutch control that you will use for your manoeuvre.

What observations should I do?

Before and during your manoeuvre, you must continually do effective observations, looking all around the car for any hazards, which may include vehicles, motorcycles, bicycles, pedestrians, etc. When you are about to start your manoeuvre, imagine your car is in the centre of a bubble that stretches six car lengths away from your car and all around the car. When any moving hazard enters the perimeter of that bubble, you should bring your car to a stop, until, either they continue out of the bubble, or they become stationary. Then you may continue your manoeuvre, ensuring the area remains safe by continual effective observations all around the car.

What is 'dry steering'?

Dry steering means turning the steering wheel without moving the car. You should try to avoid dry steering as it can damage your steering mechanism and your tyres.

What if I am going downhill?

If you are moving downhill, you may find you have to put the clutch down and control the speed of the car using the brake.

What is 'full lock'?

Full lock means turning the steering wheel as far as it goes in any one direction.

When should I select reverse gear?

When you are getting ready to perform your manoeuvre, you should prepare the car in reverse gear as soon as you can, even if you are waiting for another moving hazard to pass, as this will put on your reverse light at the back of your car, which is a signal to any hazards behind you that lets them know you are planning to reverse.

What is POM?

POM is an acronym that stands for **P**repare, **O**bserve, **M**ove. It is the order in which you should start your manoeuvre to keep it safe. We will refer to the POM routine as we go on to discuss how to perform the manoeuvre.

Turn In The Road

The turn in the road to face the other direction, is often mistakenly referred to as the three point turn. But you can perform this manoeuvre in as many turns as you need, depending on how narrow the road is. The more narrow the road, the more turns you will need to do to safely turn the car around without hitting the curb.

You may choose to do this manoeuvre if you find yourself at a dead end, or simply going the wrong way. Avoid doing this manoeuvre on a busy road, a one-way road, or a road with 'no u-turn' signs.

Hitting the curb should be avoided as you may damage your tyre, or you may mount the curb and pose a serious threat to a pedestrian. When performing a turn in the road, you should try to stop at the end of each turn, so that your car does not overhang the curb. Again, if it does, you could pose a threat to a pedestrian.

Hint: When performing this manoeuvre, if you creep very slowly and use big quick steering, you will get a tighter turn.

To keep this manoeuvre safe, you must continue to make effective observations for hazards while you are moving.

Turn In The Road

Stage One:

Prepare:

Start at the side of the road.

Prepare the car in first gear.

Find the biting point with the clutch.

Observe for Hazards:

Check middle mirror.

Check Left and right mirrors.

Look all around the car.

Check right blind spot.

Move:

Release the handbrake.

Let the car start to creep.

With big quick steers, put full lock on the steering to the right.

As you go over the centre of the road, you may find the camber of the road now slopes downhill, so you may have to put the clutch down and control the speed of the car at a creeping pace using the foot brake.

When the curb in front cuts in just under your right door mirror, stop.

Apply handbrake so you don't roll forward.

Stage Two:

Prepare:

Prepare the car in reverse gear.

Find the biting point with the clutch.

Observe for Hazards:

Check the middle mirror.

Check over right shoulder.

Look all around the car.

Look over left shoulder out of back windscreen.

Move:

Release the handbrake.

Let the car start to creep.

With big quick steers, put full lock on the steering to the left.

When you reach the centre of the road, look all around the car.

Look over your right shoulder toward the curb behind.

Remember the road may start to slope away so you may have to put the clutch down and control the speed with the brake.

When the curb behind cuts into the bottom right corner of your right window, stop.

Apply handbrake so you don't roll back.

Stage Three:

Prepare:

Prepare the car in first gear.

Find the biting point with the clutch.

Observe for Hazards:

Look all around the car.

Have a last look left for any oncoming vehicles.

Look in the direction you will be going.

Move:

Release the handbrake.

Let the car start to creep.

With big quick steers, put full lock on the steering to the right.

Keep creeping forward making sure the front of the car clears the curb in front of you. (If it is not going to clear, stop, apply handbrake, and repeat stage two and three.)

After clearing the curb in front, straighten your steering so your wheels are straight.

Check your middle and right door mirror.

If safe, drive on.

Well done. You have now completed this manoeuvre!

Reverse Parallel Park

The reverse parallel park enables you to park the car next to the curb between cars. When you park your car in this manner, ensure you have chosen a safe, legal and convenient place, and leave enough room for any parked vehicles in front or behind to be able to easily manoeuvre out from their spaces.

You should complete this entire manoeuvre within a space of two car lengths. You should start this manoeuvre at the side of the road, at a distance of about one car length behind another parked car.

If you are performing this manoeuvre on a downhill gradient, you may have to put the clutch down and use the brake to control the speed.

To keep this manoeuvre safe, you must continue to make effective observations for hazards while you are moving.

Reverse Parallel Park

Stage One:

Prepare:

Prepare the car in first gear.

Find the biting point with the clutch.

Observe for Hazards:

Check the middle mirror.

Look all around the car.

Check right blind spot.

Move:

Release the handbrake.

Let the car start to creep.

Steer to the right.

Move the car forward, around the parked car and then steer to the left until you are parallel with the parked car. Make your steering straight so your wheels are straight.

You should have a distance of 1 metre (one car door length) between the side of your car and the parked car.

Continue creeping forward until you are half way past the parked car.

Apply the handbrake.

Stage Two:

Prepare:

Prepare the car in reverse gear.

Find the biting point with the clutch.

Observe for Hazards:

Check the middle mirror.

Look all around the car.

Look over your left shoulder out of the back windscreen.

Move:

Release the handbrake.

Let the car creep straight back until it is halfway past the parked car.

Look over to your right blind spot. (This is because the front of the car is going to swing out as you continue this manoeuvre so you need to know that it is clear and safe).

Look back over your left shoulder out of the back window.

Apply full lock to the steering to the left.

Let the car creep round until you reach a 2 o'clock position.

Keep looking around the car for hazards.

Now apply full lock to the steering to the right.

Let the car creep back until it is straight behind the parked car.

Do not to get too close to the curb. (If you are getting too close to the curb, stop and move to Stage 3 A, for a correction.)

Make the steering straight so the wheels are straight.

Apply hand brake and select neutral.

Now ask yourself, have you positioned the car in a reasonable parked position within a drains width of the curb?

If yes, well done. You have completed the manoeuvre!

If no, then you need to do a correction. If you are too far away from the curb, move on to Stage 3 B for a correction.

Corrections for the Reverse Parallel Park:

Stage 3 A: If you are too close to the curb:

Prepare:

Prepare the car in first gear.

Find the biting point with the clutch.

Observe for Hazards:

Look all around the car.

Check right blind spot.

Move:

Release the handbrake.

Let the car creep forward.

Do half steer to the right.

When sufficiently away from curb, straighten the steer.

Then do half steer to the left.

When car is straight, straighten steer and stop.

Apply hand brake if on a hill.

Prepare:

Prepare the car in reverse gear.

Find biting point with the clutch.

Observe for Hazards:

Look all around the car.

Look over left shoulder out of the back windscreen.

Release the handbrake.

Let the car creep back until you are approximately one car length from the parked car.

Apply handbrake and select neutral.

Now ask yourself, have you positioned the car in a reasonable parked position within a drains width of the curb?

If yes, well done. You have completed the manoeuvre!

If no, then you need to do another correction.

Stage 3 B: If you are too far away from the curb:

Prepare:

Prepare the car in first gear.

Find the biting point with the clutch.

Observe for Hazards:

Look all around the car.

Check right blind spot.

Move:

Release the handbrake.

Let the car creep forward.

Do half steer to the left.

When sufficiently close to the curb, straighten the steer.

Then do half steer to the right.

When car is straight, straighten steer and stop.

Apply hand brake if on a hill.

Prepare:

Prepare the car in reverse gear.

Find biting point with the clutch.

Observe for Hazards:

Look all around the car.

Look over left shoulder out of the back windscreen.

Move:

Release the handbrake.

Let the car creep back until you are approximately one car length from the parked car.

Apply handbrake and select neutral.

Now ask yourself, have you positioned the car in a reasonable parked position within a drains width of the curb?

If yes, well done. You have completed the manoeuvre!

If no, then you need to do another correction.

Reverse Bay Park to the Left

This manoeuvre is designed for you to safely demonstrate how you would reverse back into a parking bay on the left, correctly positioning all four wheels of the car within the lines of the parking bay.

If you are performing this manoeuvre on a downhill gradient, you may have to put the clutch down and use the brake to control the speed.

To keep this manoeuvre safe, you must continue to make effective observations for hazards while you are moving.

Reverse Bay Park to the Left

Stage One:

Start with the car at a right angle (90') to a row of parking bays on the left.

Prepare:

Prepare the car in reverse gear.

Find the biting point with the clutch.

Observe for Hazards:

Check your right blind spot.

Look all around the car.

Look over your left shoulder out of the back windscreen.

Move:

Release the handbrake.

Let the car creep backwards.

When one of the lines that separate the bays lines up with the centre of the door on the left, look over to your right blind spot. (This is because the front of the car is going to swing out as you continue this manoeuvre so you need to know that it is clear and safe).

Apply full lock to the steering to the left.

Let the car creep round into the bay.

When the car is straight, make the steering straight so the wheels are straight.

Let the car continue to creep straight back into the bay until the front of the car is behind the line.

Apply handbrake and select neutral.

Now ask yourself, are all four wheels in the parking bay?

If yes, well done, you have completed the manoeuvre!

If no, then you need to follow the next stage to do a correction.

Corrections for the Reverse Bay Park:

Ask yourself, do you want the car to be more to the left (see Stage 2 A), or to the right (see stage 2 B)?

Stage 2 A:

If you want the car to be more to the left:

Prepare:

Prepare the car in first gear.

Find the biting point with the clutch.

Observe for Hazards:

Look all around the car for any hazards.

Move:

Release the handbrake.

Let the car creep forward.

Put half steer to the left.

When car has moved sufficiently to the left, straighten the steering.

Now do half steer to the right.

When car is straight, steer straight so the wheels are straight.

Stop and apply handbrake if you are on a hill.

If you have moved the car over enough, you should be able to see the lines either side of the bay you are aiming for in your door mirrors.

Prepare:

Now prepare the car in reverse gear.

Find the biting point with the clutch.

Observe for Hazards:

Look all around the car.

Look over your left shoulder out of the back windscreen.

Move:

Release the handbrake.

Let the car creep straight back into the bay.

Stop when the front of the car is behind the line.

Apply handbrake and select neutral.

Now ask yourself, are all four wheels in the parking bay?

If yes, well done, you have completed the manoeuvre!

If no, then you need to do another correction. Refer back to Stage 2 A, or Stage 2 B.

Stage 2 B:

If you want the car to be more to the right:

Prepare:

Prepare the car in first gear.

Find the biting point with the clutch.

Observe for Hazards:

Look all around the car for any hazards.

Move:

Release the handbrake.

Let the car creep forward.

Put half steer to the right.

When car has moved sufficiently to the right, straighten the steering.

Now do half steer to the left.

When car is straight, steer straight so the wheels are straight.

Stop and apply handbrake if you are on a hill.

If you have moved the car over enough, you should be able to see the lines either side of the bay you are aiming for in your door mirrors.

Prepare:

Now prepare the car in reverse gear.

Find the biting point with the clutch.

Observe for Hazards:

Look all around the car.

Look over your left shoulder out of the back windscreen.

Move:

Release the handbrake.

Let the car creep straight back into the bay.

Stop when the front of the car is behind the line.

Apply handbrake and select neutral.

Now ask yourself, are all four wheels in the parking bay?

If yes, well done, you have completed the manoeuvre!

If no, then you need to do another correction. Refer back to Stage 2 A, or stage 2 B.

Reverse Bay Park to the Right

This manoeuvre is designed for you to safely demonstrate how you would reverse back into a parking bay on the right, correctly positioning all four wheels of the car within the lines of the parking bay.

If you are performing this manoeuvre on a downhill gradient, you may have to put the clutch down and use the brake to control the speed.

To keep this manoeuvre safe, you must continue to make effective observations for hazards while you are moving.

Reverse Bay Park to the Right

Stage One:

Start with the car at a right angle (90') to a row of parking bays on the right.

Prepare:

Prepare the car in reverse gear.

Find the biting point with the clutch.

Observe for Hazards:

Check your right blind spot.

Look all around the car.

Look over your left shoulder out of the back windscreen.

Move:

Release the handbrake.

Let the car creep backwards.

When one of the lines that separate the bays lines up with the centre of the door on the right, look all around the car. (This is because the front of the car is going to swing out as you continue this manoeuvre so you need to know that it is clear and safe).

Apply full lock to the steering to the right.

Let the car creep round into the bay.

When the car is straight, make the steering straight so the wheels are straight.

Let the car continue to creep straight back into the bay until the front of the car is behind the line.

Apply handbrake and select neutral.

Now ask yourself, are all four wheels in the parking bay?

If yes, well done, you have completed the manoeuvre!

If no, then you need to follow the next stage to do a correction.

Corrections for the Reverse Bay Park:

Ask yourself, do you want the car to be more to the left (see Stage 2 A), or to the right (see stage 2 B)?

Stage 2 A:

If you want the car to be more to the left:

Prepare:

Prepare the car in first gear.

Find the biting point with the clutch.

Observe for Hazards:

Look all around the car for any hazards.

Move:

Release the handbrake.

Let the car creep forward.

Put half steer to the left.

When car has moved sufficiently to the left, straighten the steering.

Now do half steer to the right.

When car is straight, steer straight so the wheels are straight.

Stop and apply handbrake if you are on a hill.

If you have moved the car over enough, you should be able to see the lines either side of the bay you are aiming for in your door mirrors.

Prepare:

Now prepare the car in reverse gear.

Find the biting point with the clutch.

Observe for Hazards:

Look all around the car.

Look over your left shoulder out of the back windscreen.

Move:

Release the handbrake.

Let the car creep straight back into the bay.

Stop when the front of the car is behind the line.

Apply handbrake and select neutral.

Now ask yourself, are all four wheels in the parking bay?

If yes, well done, you have completed the manoeuvre!

If no, then you need to do another correction. Refer back to Stage 2 A, or Stage 2 B.

Stage 2 B:

If you want the car to be more to the right:

Prepare:

Prepare the car in first gear.

Find the biting point with the clutch.

Observe for Hazards:

Look all around the car for any hazards.

Move:

Release the handbrake.

Let the car creep forward.

Put half steer to the right.

When car has moved sufficiently to the right, straighten the steering.

Now do half steer to the left.

When car is straight, steer straight so the wheels are straight.

Stop and apply handbrake if you are on a hill.

If you have moved the car over enough, you should be able to see the lines either side of the bay you are aiming for in your door mirrors.

Prepare:

Now prepare the car in reverse gear.

Find the biting point with the clutch.

Observe for Hazards:

Look all around the car.

Look over your left shoulder out of the back windscreen.

Move:

Release the handbrake.

Let the car creep straight back into the bay.

Stop when the front of the car is behind the line.

Apply handbrake and select neutral.

Now ask yourself, are all four wheels in the parking bay?

If yes, well done, you have completed the manoeuvre!

If no, then you need to do another correction. Refer back to Stage 2 A, or stage 2 B.

Left Reverse Around the Corner

This manoeuvre is designed for you to safely change the direction you are travelling in if you find you are going the wrong way.

If you are moving downhill, you may find you have to put the clutch down and control the speed of the car using the brake.

Before you do this manoeuvre, look closely at the curve you will be reversing around and ask yourself, how tight is the curb? Will it require half a steer, three quarter steer or one full steer? The tighter the curve, the more steer it will require.

To keep this manoeuvre safe, you must continue to make effective observations for hazards while you are moving.

Left reverse Around the Corner

Stage One:

Prepare:

Start on the left side of the road, with the road that you wish to reverse into in front of you.

Prepare the car in first gear.

Find the biting point with the clutch.

Observe for Hazards:

Check middle mirror.

Look all around the car.

Check right blind spot.

Move:

Move away from the side of the road.

Drive across and past the road you wish to reverse into.

As you drive past, look into the road for any hazards such as parked cars, skips, children playing etc, which may mean you will have to find an alternative road to reverse into.

If the road you are driving past is clear, check middle mirror and left mirror.

If safe, pull up on the left, about two car lengths past the road and about a drains width from the curb. A signal will only be required if it will benefit another road user.

Apply handbrake.

Stage 2:

Hint: have a look over your left shoulder out of the back windscreen to see where the curb behind cuts into the car. This point is your straight line reference point. Remembering this reference point will help you when you perform your manoeuvre as it shows you how close to the curb you should be.

Prepare:

Select reverse gear.

Find the biting point with the clutch.

Observe for Hazards:

Look all around the car.

Look over your left shoulder out of the back windscreen.

Move:

Let the car start to creep.

Keep the car straight until the straight part of the curb of the new road you will be reversing into lines up with the bottom left corner of your back left window.

Now look over to your right blind spot. (This is because the front of the car is going to swing out as you continue this manoeuvre so you need to know that it is clear and safe).

Look back over your left shoulder out of the back window.

Now steer to the left. How much steer will depend on how tight the curve of the curb is. Will it require half a steer, three quarter steer or one full steer? The tighter the curve, the more steer it will require.

Let the car creep around the curb into the new road.

When the car is straight in the new road, make the steering straight so the wheels are straight.

Remember: you must continue to make effective observations for hazards while you are moving!

Now look over your left shoulder out of the back windscreen.

Continue to let the car creep back.

Now look for your straight line reference point and follow instruction **A** or instruction **B**.

A: If the curb is left of the straight line reference point, then quarter steer to left.

When straight line reference point lines up with the curb, then quarter steer to the right.

When car is straight, make steering straight so wheels are straight.

B: If the curb is right of the straight line reference point, then quarter steer to right.

When straight line reference point lines up with the curb, then quarter steer to the left.

When car is straight, make steering straight so wheels are straight.

Continue reversing, keeping curb lined up with your straight line reference point until you have moved three car lengths back from the give way line.

Bring the car to a stop.

Apply handbrake and select neutral.

You should have finished within a drains width of the curb.

Well done, you have completed this manoeuvre!

Correction for Left Reverse Around the Corner:

If at any time during this manoeuvre you find that you are too close to the curb, you must stop. You should not hit the curb or you may damage your tyres and if you mount the curb you could be a threat to any pedestrians.

Prepare:

Prepare the car in first gear.

Find the biting point with the clutch.

Observe for Hazards:

Look all around the car.

Check your right blind spot.

Move:

Let the car creep forward and do half steer to right moving the car away from the curb.

When car has moved sufficiently away, do half steer to the left.

When car is straight, make the steering straight so the wheels are straight.

Now you may continue your reversing manoeuvre.

Prepare:

Prepare the care in reverse gear.

Find the biting point with the clutch.

Observe for Hazards:

Look all around the car.

Look over left shoulder out of back windscreen.

Move:

Let the car creep back and continue the manoeuvre as per previous instructions.

Well done, you have completed the correction!

Right Reverse Around the corner

This manoeuvre is designed for you to safely change the direction you are travelling in if you find you are going the wrong way.

If you are moving downhill, you may find you have to put the clutch down and control the speed of the car using the brake.

Before you do this manoeuvre, look closely at the curve you will be reversing around and ask yourself, how tight is the curb? Will it require half a steer, three quarter steer or one full steer? The tighter the curve, the more steer it will require.

To keep this manoeuvre safe, you must continue to make effective observations for hazards while you are moving.

Right Reverse Around the Corner

Stage One:

Prepare:

Start on the left side of the road, with the road that you wish to reverse into in front of you on the right.

Prepare the car in first gear.

Find the biting point with the clutch.

Observe for Hazards:

Check middle mirror.

Look all around the car.

Check right blind spot.

Move:

Move away from the side of the road.

Check your middle mirror.

Check your right door mirror.

If safe, when you are half way past the road on your right, put your right signal on.

Move across the road.

As you drive past, look into the road on the right for any hazards such as parked cars, skips, children playing etc, which may mean you will have to find an alternative road to reverse into.

Pull up on the right side of your road, about two car lengths past the road on the right.

You should be a drains width away from the curb.

Apply handbrake.

Stage 2:

Hint: have a look over your left shoulder out of the back windscreen to see where the curb behind cuts into the car. This point is your straight line reference point. Remembering this reference point will help you when you perform your manoeuvre as it shows you how close to the curb you should be.

Prepare:

Select reverse gear.

Find the biting point with the clutch.

Observe for Hazards:

Look all around the car.

Look over your left shoulder out of the back windscreen.

Move:

Let the car start to creep.

Move the car straight back.

Keep looking from your left to your right shoulder and back.

When curb on right starts to drop away from the back right wheel of the car, steer to the right. How much steer will depend on how tight the curve of the curb is. Will it require half a steer, three quarter steer or one full steer? The tighter the curve, the more steer it will require.

When the car is straight in the new road make the steering straight so the wheels are straight.

Now look over your left shoulder for your straight line reference point and follow instruction **A** or instruction **B**.

A: If the curb is left of the straight line reference point, then quarter steer to left.

When straight line reference point lines up with the curb, then quarter steer to the right.

When car is straight, make steering straight so wheels are straight.

B: If the curb is right of the straight line reference point, then quarter steer to right.

When straight line reference point lines up with the curb, then quarter steer to the left.

When car is straight, make steering straight so wheels are straight.

Continue reversing, keeping curb lined up with your straight line reference point until you have moved five car lengths back from the give way line.

Bring the car to a stop.

Apply handbrake and select neutral.

You should have finished within a drains width of the curb.

Well done, you have completed this manoeuvre!

Correction for Right Reverse Around the Corner:

If at any time during this manoeuvre you find that you are too close to the curb, you must stop. You should not hit the curb or you may damage your tyres and if you mount the curb you could be a threat to any pedestrians.

Prepare:

Prepare the car in first gear.

Find the biting point with the clutch.

Observe for Hazards:

Look all around the car.

Check your left blind spot.

Move:

Let the car creep forward and do half steer to left moving the car away from the curb.

When car has moved sufficiently away, do half steer to the right.

When car is straight, make the steering straight so the wheels are straight.

Now you may continue your reversing manoeuvre.

Prepare:

Prepare the care in reverse gear.

Find the biting point with the clutch.

Observe for Hazards:

Look all around the car.

Look over left shoulder out of back windscreen.

Move:

Let the car creep back and continue the manoeuvre as per previous instructions.

Well done, you have completed the correction!

Emergency Stop

Whilst driving normally, you should be checking your middle mirror at least every five seconds. If you see a warning sign, warning you of a hazard, you should check your middle mirror so that you know the true distance and speed of vehicles behind you. It may also be sensible to reduce your speed, especially if you see a vehicle is too close behind you in this circumstance. These actions will reduce your chances of needing to do an emergency stop and will give the vehicle behind you more time to react if you do have to stop suddenly.

When performing an emergency stop, you must react quickly.

You may find the anti-lock braking system (ABS) comes on if you car has this system. This serves to stop the wheels from locking up during harsh braking. If it does come on, you may feel a judder under your foot in the brake pedal, and the car may be making a grinding noise. Do not worry... you have not broken anything! Just keep braking.

If your car does not have ABS, and the wheels lock up during harsh braking, then release and reapply the brake pedal, and continue to do so until the wheels unlock. This is called cadence braking.

Very rarely, you may find the car will begin to skid. If the back of the car skids to the left, you should steer to the left to allow the wheels to re-grip the road. Similarly, if the back of the car skids to the right, you should steer to the right to allow the wheels to re-grip the road.

Emergency Stop

Stage One:

You will be driving normally.

Now, imagine a child has run out in front of your car.

You should already have been checking your mirror at least every five seconds so you should already know what is behind you. You do not want to waste time checking your mirror now.

Keep looking ahead of you.

Keep your steering straight.

With quick reactions, press firmly down on your brake pedal.

Press your clutch to the floor.

Keep both feet down on both pedals until the car has come to a stop.

Apply the handbrake.

Select Neutral.

Now you can relax your feet off the pedals.

Stage Two:

Now imagine there will be a mum and other people running towards the child to see if he is ok. They may be coming from any direction around your car.

Prepare

Prepare the car in first gear.

Find the biting point with the clutch.

Observe for Hazards

You must look all around the car from left to right for any hazards.

Move

If it is safe, drive on.

Well done. You have completed this manoeuvre!

Conclusion

I hope you have been able to use this guide to enhance your control, observation and accuracy while performing your manoeuvres. I have aimed to deconstruct each manoeuvre into sets of simple step by step instructions in order to maximise understanding.

I also hope that when you have passed your driving test and are driving independently, that you will continue to apply the information in this guide to keep yourself and other road users safe.

My final two pieces of advice will be those that have correctly and continually re-occurred throughout this guide:

1. While performing any manoeuvre, you must continue to make effective observations for hazards both before and while you are moving.

2. The slower you perform the manoeuvre, the easier it becomes, as you give yourself time to be more accurate with your thinking and steering.

So go slow and look everywhere!

Supplementary Bonus:

Show Me Tell Me Questions

Below is a list of the Show Me Tell Me questions, two of which will be asked on your driving test.

Q: Show me how you would check that the direction indicators are working.
A: Apply the hazard warning switch, walk around the car and check the functioning of all indicator bulbs.

Q: Tell me how you would check that the brakes are working before starting a journey.
A: Applying pressure to the brake pedal, it should not feel spongy or slack. Brakes should be tested as you set off, the vehicle should not pull to one side.

Q: Tell me where the windscreen washer reservoir is and tell me how you would check the windscreen washer level.
A: Identify reservoir and explain how to check level. If there is no level gauge then top up regularly.

Q: Show me how you would check that the brake lights are working on this car. (I can assist you. You need to switch the ignition on, please don't start the engine)
A: Switch on the ignition (Do NOT start the engine) Apply pressure to the brake pedal, ask the examiner to check the bulbs. (If alone you can make use of reflections in windows, garage doors, etc.)

Q: Show me and explain how you would check that the power assisted steering is working before starting a journey.
A: Apply gentle pressure to the steering wheel, wheel should be stiff. Maintain pressure while the engine is started, the wheel should become looser and easier to move.(Avoid dry steering)

Q: Tell me where you would find the information for the recommended tyre pressures for this car and how tyre pressures should be checked.
A: Pressures are found in the manufacturer's guide. Using a reliable pressure gauge, check the pressures when tyres are cold, remembering the spare tyre.

Q: Show me how you would check the parking brake (handbrake) for excessive wear, make sure you keep safe control of the vehicle.
A: Keep control by firmly applying the footbrake. Release the parking brake (handbrake) and then reapply it fully ensuring it secures itself, and is not at the end of the working travel.

Q: Open the bonnet, and tell me where you would check the engine oil level and tell me how you would check that the engine has sufficient oil.
A: Identify the dipstick, remove it. Clean the dipstick, replace it. Remove the dipstick and check of oil level against the

minimum/maximum markers, and do this when the engine is cold.

Q: Open the bonnet, tell me where you would check the engine coolant level and tell me how you would check that the engine has the correct level.
A: Locate the engine coolant. Check level using the gauge on the side.

Q: Tell me how you make sure your head restraint is correctly adjusted so it provides the best protection in the event of a crash.
A: The head restraint should be adjusted so the rigid/centre part of the head restraint is level with your eyes and ears, and as close to the back of the head as is comfortable.

Q: Open the bonnet, Tell me where the brake fluid reservoir is and tell me how you would check that you have a safe level of hydraulic brake fluid.
A: Locate the reservoir (Look for the (O) brake symbol), check level against Max/Min markings.

Q: Tell me how you would check the tyres to ensure that they have sufficient tread depth and that their general condition is safe to use on the road.
A: Ensure that there are no cuts and bulges, Tread depth should be 1.6mm across the central ¾ (75%) of the tyre, and all the way round the tyre.

Q: Show me how you would check that the horn is working (off road only).
A: Apply pressure to the horn (this is permitted in test centre car parks).

Q: Show me how you would clean the windscreen using the windscreen washer and wipers.
A: Operate the control to wash and clear windscreen (turn ignition on if necessary).

Q: Tell me how you would check that the headlights & tail lights are working. (No need to exit vehicle).
A: Switch on your headlights. Tell the examiner "Turn on the lights, then walk

round vehicle." (Note: this is a "Tell Me" question, there is no need to physically exit the vehicle to check the lights.)

Q: Show me how you would set the demister controls to clear all the windows effectively, this should include both front and rear screens.
A: Set all relevant controls including; fan, temperature, air direction and heated screen to clear windscreen and windows. You may need to start the engine.

Q: Show me how you would switch on the fog light(s) and explain when you would use it/them. (No need to exit vehicle).
A: Turn on dipped headlights. Turn on fog light switch. Check warning light is on. Lights should be used when visibility is less than 100 metres.

Q: Tell me how you would know if there was a problem with your anti-lock braking system (ABS).
A: An ABS warning light should illuminate if there is a fault.

Q: Show me how you switch your headlight from dipped to main beam and explain how you would know the main beam is on whilst inside the car.

A: Switch on the main beam, check using the warning light.